NUMBER KIT 3

Ideas to the rescue

Number facts

All rights reserved. This book is sold subject to the condition that it shall not, by way of trade or otherwise, be lent, hired out or otherwise circulated without the publisher's prior consent in any form of binding or cover other than that in which it is published and without a similar condition, including this condition, being imposed upon the subsequent purchaser.

No part of this publication may be reproduced, stored in a retrieval system, or transmitted, in any form or by any means, electronic, mechanical, photocopying, recording or otherwise, without the prior permission of the publisher. This book remains copyright, although permission is granted to copy those pages labelled PHOTOCOPIABLE for classroom distribution and use only in the school which has purchased the book, or by the teacher who has purchased this book, and in accordance with the CLA licensing agreement. Photocopying permission is given for purchasers only and not for borrowers of books from any lending service.

British Library Cataloguing-in-Publication Data
A catalogue record for this book is available from the British Library.

ISBN 0-590-53589-7

Published by Scholastic Ltd
Villiers House
Clarendon Avenue
Leamington Spa
Warwickshire CV32 5PR

© 1996 Scholastic Ltd
123456789 6789012345

AUTHOR
June Loewenstein

SERIES CONSULTANT
Sheila Ebbutt
Director of BEAM (Be A Mathematician) which is supported by Islington Council

CURRICULUM LINKS
Ian Gardner, Maths Curriculum Adviser (England and Wales), Megan Emmerson, with Edinburgh Centre for Mathematics Education (Scotland) and Michael Wallace (Northern Ireland)

The publishers wish to thank the following individuals and organisations for their invaluable help in developing the *Maths Focus* concept: Jayne de Courcy, Courcy Consultants; Dr Daphne Kerslake; The Mathematics Centre, Chichester Institute of Higher Education; Oxfordshire Maths Centre; Edinburgh Centre for Mathematics Education; David Bell, Chief Education Officer, City of Newcastle-upon-Tyne; Professor Geoffrey and Dr Julia Matthews.

EDITORIAL TEAM
Angela Dewsbury, Joel Lane and Libby Weaver

SERIES DESIGNER
Joy White

DESIGNERS
Blade Communications

COVER PHOTOGRAPH
© Scott Campbell for Scholastic Inc.

ILLUSTRATORS
John Blakeman, Kim Blundell (John Martin & Artists Ltd.), Mik Brown (Kathy Jakeman Illustration), Andy Hamond (Garden Studio), Pat McCarthy, Liz McIntosh (Linda Rogers Associates), Rachael O'Neill (Kathy Jakeman Illustration), Fred Pipes, Jon Riley, William Rudling (John Martin & Artists Ltd)

POSTERMAT
Pat McCarthy

Designed using Aldus Pagemaker
Processed by PAGES Bureau, Leamington Spa
Printed in Great Britain by Ebenezer Baylis & Son, Worcester and George Over, Rugby

© Material from the National Curriculum, Scottish 5–14 Guidelines and the Northern Ireland Curriculum is Crown copyright and is reproduced by permission of the Controller of HMSO, 1995.

ACKNOWLEDGEMENT
Thanks to **Walker Books Ltd** for the use of text and illustration adaptation from *Christmas in Exeter Street* by Diana Hendry, illustrations © 1989 John Lawrence, text © 1989 Diana Hendry (1989, Walker Books Ltd)

CONTENTS

4	*MATHS FOCUS* OFFERS
6	HERE'S THE MATHS
8	CURRICULUM LINKS
9	USING AND APPLYING GRID

DIAGNOSTIC ASSESSMENT
10	BAGS AND BAGS OF MARBLES

ASSESSMENT DOUBLE-CHECK
14	A TRIP DOWN THE STREET

REINFORCEMENT ACTIVITIES
16	BACK TO ZERO!
18	10S AND 100S GAME
20	CAKE SHOP
22	SWIMMING FOR GOLD
24	FOREST LUNCH
26	THE WIZARD'S NAME
28	GREAT MOTORCYCLE RACE 1
30	SECRET OF THE NINES

ENRICHMENT ACTIVITIES
32	SPEND! SPEND! SPEND!
34	999
36	EASTER AT EXETER STREET
38	KIOSK ON THE BEACH
40	GREAT MOTORCYCLE RACE 2
42	TARGET PRACTICE

RESOURCES
44	10S AND 100S CARDS
45	GREAT MOTORCYCLE RACE 1
46	999 CARDS
47	GREAT MOTORCYCLE RACE 2
48	PHOTOCOPIABLE OF POSTERMAT

MATHS FOCUS

Maths Focus can be used to:

- assess children's knowledge and skills;
- offer reinforcement activities to develop understanding;
- provide enrichment activities to consolidate and extend the learning;
- develop skills and ability in using and applying mathematics.

DIFFERENTIATION

1 Maths Focus offers structured progression of content and skills through the Kits 1–5* and provides links with all UK national curricula. With a particular class or year group, you may use activities from more than one kit to cater for all ability levels. Each book focuses on a specific mathematical concept, with activities set in a range of contexts – including games, stories, problems, everyday situations and puzzles – so that children learn to use their mathematics flexibly and appropriately.

2 Assessment activities allow you to evaluate the children's ability to use and apply the mathematics they have learned.

3 Understanding is developed through two types of activity:
- **Reinforcement activities** – which increase children's confidence by concentrating on a specific concept or skill and presenting the maths in a variety of contexts;
- **Enrichment activities** – which consolidate and extend children's learning in more open-ended contexts.

4 Extension ideas at the end of each activity offer ways for more able children to go further in their exploration of a concept.

*See inside back cover for overview of kits and curriculum coverage.

offers...

FLEXIBLE RESOURCE

Maths Focus can be used in a variety of ways to support your teaching of mathematics and your style of teaching, allowing you to use the activities with individuals, groups or the whole class.

Use *Maths Focus* activities alongside a published scheme to:
- develop children's understanding of specific concepts in a greater range of contexts;
- assess children's understanding of a concept, and then to support or extend it with differentiated activities;
- focus on the using and applying aspect of the mathematics curriculum.

If you don't use a published scheme use *Maths Focus*:
- as a core resource when planning your own scheme of work;
- to teach and assess specific concepts.

USING & APPLYING

Aspects of **Using and Applying** covered by each activity are given in the teachers' notes. To help with your planning, the grid on page 9 and the teachers' notes highlight how problem solving, communication and logical reasoning are built into each activity.

USING TALK

All teachers' notes pages offer questions you can ask children to encourage them to talk about what they are doing. Use the questions while they are working to focus their mathematical thinking or at the end of the activity to assess their level of understanding. Most pages also offer:
- **Here's the maths** – explanations of the maths included in the activity;
- **What to look for** – diagnostic pointers to help you to assess whether the child has achieved the mathematical aim of the activity;
- **More help needed** – ways to help children are who struggling with the activity.

ASSESSMENT

Maths Focus offers two types of assessment to be used when you feel appropriate to plan the best way forward for each child.

- You may want to use the **Diagnostic assessment** activity at the start of teaching a concept to establish the existing level of understanding. Alternatively, use it after some initial teaching, to provide a check on progress.

- The **Assessment double-check** allows you to assess the child's understanding of the concept as a whole, to see how their learning has progressed.

RANGE OF RESOURCES

Maths Focus kits come with a full-colour laminated postermat for each book. This flexible wipe-clean resource can be used with a number of the activities in its book and also as a general mathematics resource. Each book has a black and white photocopiable version of its postermat, to use with the activities and for permanent recording of the children's work. Extra postermats are available separately (see inside back cover).

The activities in each book are planned to use a range of mathematical resources, including counting apparatus, number lines and grids and calculators. Mental maths is emphasised throughout.

Being able to calculate in your head is a valuable skill. Children will have their own ways of visualising the calculations. We can introduce them to various mental maths strategies to help them decide which to use.

Here's the maths ...

Knowing number facts

What's involved

Mental maths

▶ There are many strategies we can use to carry out calculations in our heads. We all develop and adapt our own methods.

▶ There are various ways we can help children to develop methods which work for them. These include:
- encouraging them to become familiar with various number patterns and to use calculators to explore these patterns;
- making counting materials and number lines available, so that they can model their calculations to help them move from the concrete to the abstract (visualising the method);
- providing them with meaningful contexts which require them to use their skills of quick number recall.

▶ Children need to realise the importance of good recording. They need to record their calculations in a way that they understand and that communicates their method to others. Let them choose their own method of recording; discussing different methods will allow children to see ways of modifying their own methods to make them more effective (if necessary).

▶ Children need to start from the concrete, modelling a problem in practical terms, before they move on to the abstract. Encourage them to reconstruct in their heads the practical way they have carried out a calculation. Get them to discuss their mental images of the model used, so that they can visualise it in order to carry out new calculations in their heads.

Different strategies

▶ Children should be introduced to different mental strategies, and then left to adapt and use the methods they

PATTERNS

▶ Recognising and using number patterns is of tremendous help to children in mental calculation.

▶ Knowing and understanding, for example, that if 10 is added to a number the unit digit stays the same, that multiplying by 5 must give an answer ending in 5 or zero, and that adding an odd number to an even number must give an odd answer, will be invaluable for mental calculations.

▶ Children can use this knowledge to achieve more efficient mental calculations. We need to give them activities which allow them to develop this knowledge in meaningful contexts.

MENTAL AGILITY

▶ As well as helping children to acquire mental strategies, we need to give them practice in recall.

▶ Activities involving quick mental recall, for small groups of children of similar ability, can be enjoyable and provide invaluable practice in consolidating existing number fact knowledge. For example, let them play a game such as 'Four steps to 100', where

IDEAS TO THE RESCUE
MATHS FOCUS – NUMBER KIT 3

RESOURCES TO USE

Counting materials
◗ Counting materials can help children who are having difficulty with the abstract nature of number to 'see' what is going on. After all, it was through counting materials that the children's first understanding of number was developed.
◗ For example, counters and fingers provide concrete models that are useful for calculations involving small numbers. Structural apparatus, such as Cuisenaire rods and base 10 blocks, will help with calculations involving larger numbers by showing children how such numbers can be combined. The abacus helps with the understanding of place value.

Number lines
◗ Number lines help children to appreciate the idea of ordinal number: the order in which the number names come in a counting sequence. Addition and subtraction can be illustrated by moving forwards and backwards along the line. Multiples can be shown by making equal jumps along the line, starting from zero. Number lines also help children to form mental images, for example when performing 'shopkeeper's addition' (subtraction). To solve 30 – 16, some children (and indeed many adults) count on from 16 to 30.

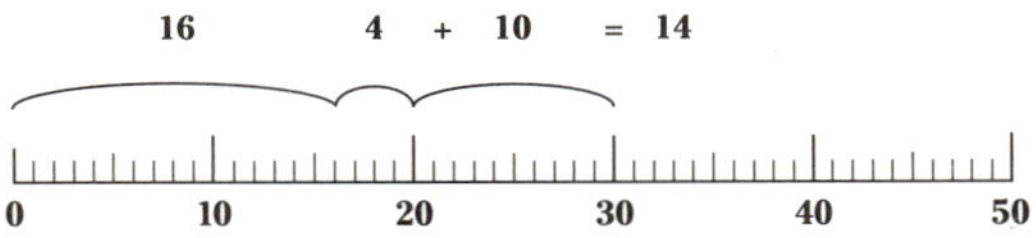

16   4 + 10   = 14
|————|——————|
0   10   20   30   40   50

Calculators
◗ Calculators should not just be used as a device for checking. They provide an invaluable way of exploring the number patterns that help children to develop a firm understanding of number and of techniques for calculation. For example, when 9 is added repeatedly to any number, it can be seen that the tens go up by one each time while the units go down by one. This pattern might well be forgotten in the effort to do the sums, whereas seeing it develop quickly on the calculator is exciting and gives children an incentive to investigate further. It is important to encourage the children to discuss what they have discovered.

understand best and are most comfortable with.
◗ For example, there are several mental strategies for subtracting 18. These include:
• subtracting ten first and then eight;
• subtracting eight first and then ten;
• subtracting twenty and then adding two;
• adding on from eighteen to the number it is being subtracted from ('shopkeepers' addition').
◗ Encourage children to share the mental methods they use with others and compare them. Explaining a method will also help to reinforce the child's understanding of it. This process should be part of any activity involving calculations – it is important not to focus solely on getting the 'right' answer.

from any starting point they have to find four additions which will take them to 100. Starting from 37, for example, they could give '37 + 3 + 20 + 15 + 25'.

KEY FACTS

◗ Knowledge of number patterns can help children with mental calculation.
◗ Modelling a calculation can help children to move from the physical to the abstract and be able to 'see' it in their heads.
◗ Recording what they do helps to consolidate children's understanding of the strategy they have used.

KEY WORDS

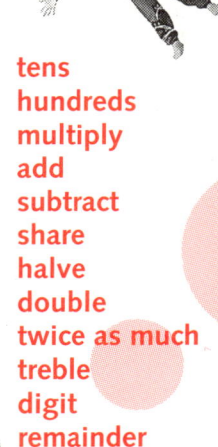

tens
hundreds
multiply
add
subtract
share
halve
double
twice as much
treble
digit
remainder

IDEAS TO THE RESCUE
MATHS FOCUS – NUMBER KIT 3

Curriculum links

This chart outlines the particular strands and statements from each of the UK curriculum documents for maths that apply to the content of this book.

The processes outlined opposite show how this maths is applied to a range of contexts and how outcomes are reported.

MATHEMATICS IN THE NATIONAL CURRICULUM (ENGLAND AND WALES)

This book covers the following statements from the Key Stage 2 Programme of Study for Number:
▶ Pupils should be given opportunities to:
• develop flexible and effective methods of computation and recording, and use them with understanding;
• use calculators... as tools for exploring number structure and to enable work with realistic data. (1a, b [part])
Pupils should be taught to:
▶ Develop an understanding of place value and extend the number system
• read, write and order whole numbers, understanding that the position of a digit signifies its value; use their understanding of place value to develop methods of computation, to approximate numbers to the nearest 10 or 100. (2a [part])
▶ Understand relationships between numbers and develop methods of computation
• explore number sequences, *e.g. counting in different sizes of step, doubling and halving, using a multiplication square,* explaining patterns and using simple relationships;
• consolidate knowledge of addition and subtraction facts to 20;
• understand multiplication as repeated addition, and division as sharing and repeated subtraction;
• understand and use the relationships between the four operations, including inverses;
• understand and use the features of a basic calculator, interpreting the display in the context of the problem, including rounding and remainders. (3a [part], c [part], e [part], f, h)
▶ Solve numerical problems
• develop their use of the four operations to solve problems, including those involving money and measures, using a calculator where appropriate;
• choose sequences of methods of computation appropriate to a problem, adapt them and apply them accurately. (4a, b)

Since this book is relevant to the middle primary years, the activities may be found to overlap between the above Key Stage 2 areas and similar areas at Key Stage 1.

MATHEMATICS 5–14 (SCOTTISH GUIDELINES)

This book covers the following strands of the Attainment Outcome Number, Money and Measurement:
▶ Add and subtract:
• **Add and subtract:** mentally for numbers 0 to 20, and in some cases beyond 20; without a calculator for two-digit numbers; in applications in number, measurement and money, including payments and change up to £1. (Level B)
▶ Multiply and divide:
• **Multiply and divide:** mentally by 2, 3, 4, 5, 10, within the confines of these tables; without a calculator for two-digit numbers multiplied by 2, 3, 4, 5, 10; in applications in number, measurement and money to £1. (Level B)

NORTHERN IRELAND CURRICULUM FOR MATHEMATICS

This book covers this strand of Number from the Programme of Study for Mathematics at Key Stage 1:
▶ Operations and their application
Pupils should have opportunities to:
(a) understand the operations of addition and subtraction...; add and subtract, initially using small numbers and progressing to working with hundreds, tens and units; use these skills to solve problems involving whole numbers;
(b) progress to understanding the operations of multiplication and division and use them to solve problems with whole numbers...;
(c) know addition and subtraction facts, initially to 10 and then to 20; ...know multiplication tables relating to the 2s, 5s, 10s and other tables, as appropriate; use these facts in problem-solving situations.

IDEAS TO THE RESCUE
MATHS FOCUS – NUMBER KIT 3

Using and applying

All of the activities in **Maths Focus** involve applying mathematics. This chart will help you to identify which strands of Using and Applying Mathematics are part of each activity. Problem-solving and Enquiry (Scottish 5–14 Guidelines) and Processes (NI Curriculum) are also addressed through these statements.

Activities	Problem Solving	Communication	Logical Reasoning
DIAGNOSTIC ASSESSMENT			
Bags and bags of marbles	Work independently. Work systematically. Check results. Select the appropriate mathematics. Use materials appropriately.	Record appropriately. Explain the results.	Show understanding of number patterns. Show understanding of the relationship between multiplication and division.
ASSESSMENT DOUBLE-CHECK			
A trip down the street	Know how to tackle the questions. Select appropriate cards. Find some or all of the answers.	Commmunicate effectively in a group situation. Represent findings in an appropriate way.	Organise the work effectively. Check the work and use approximation to check the reasonableness of answers.
REINFORCEMENT ACTIVITIES			
Back to zero!	Work systematically.	Discuss findings using mathematical language. Record accurately.	Predict successful jump sizes.
10s and 100s game	Approach the task systematically.	Discuss and account for errors.	Understand the reasons for the results and the connections with place value.
Cake shop	Develop a mental strategy for subtraction.	Explain how to give the change, using the number line.	Appreciate that the more money is spent, the less change there will be.
Swimming for gold		Describe the number patterns.	Use number pattern knowledge to find the missing numbers.
Forest lunch	Check answers.	Use language associated with doubling and halving. Explain how to halve numbers.	See that doubling makes a number larger and halving makes it smaller.
The wizard's name	Use own method to find the missing numbers. Devise own problems.		Understand the reasoning behind inverse operations.
Great motorcycle race 1	Check the answers.	Discuss disputed answers before checking. Use mathematical language correctly.	Use number pattern knowledge to assist mental recall of number facts.
Secret of the nines	Use mental maths to find numbers divisible by 9 with no remainder. Organise the task to work systematically.	Record accurately. Explain any findings.	Spot a pattern in the numbers.
ENRICHMENT ACTIVITIES			
Spend! Spend! Spend!	Work systematically. Develop mental strategies. Check results.	Discuss the work. Record clearly and systematically.	
999	Apply known strategies.	Discuss mental methods used.	
Easter at Exeter Street	Work systematically. Use and develop mental strategies. Check results.	Discuss the work. Record clearly and systematically.	Think ahead to reach the solution more quickly.
Kiosk on the beach	Use the mental strategy given to work out the bills.	Discuss the work Record clearly.	Know when an answer is reasonable or not.
Great motorcycle race 2	Use counting materials to check answers.	Discuss disputed answers before checking. Use appropriate mathematical language.	Use number pattern knowledge to assist mental recall of number facts.
Target practice	Devise own strategies. Work systematically. Check scores.	Discuss strategies used. Record clearly.	Recognise the number patterns involved.

IDEAS TO THE RESCUE
MATHS FOCUS – NUMBER KIT 3

DIAGNOSTIC ASSESSMENT

Bags and bags of marbles

Key aims
▶ To discover whether the child is able to:
• use knowledge of addition and subtraction facts to 20;
• use knowledge of multiplication facts;
• select the appropriate mathematics.

What you need
▶ 1 activity sheet 'Bags and bags of marbles 1' and 1 activity sheet 'Bags and bags of marbles 2' per child
▶ pencils
▶ counting materials

Organisation
▶ Have counting materials available for those children who want them.

The activities
▶ Show the group the first activity sheet 'Bags and bags of marbles 1', and talk through what is involved.
▶ Ask them to suggest possible ways to fill the two bags, making sure there are 20 marbles in each bag. For example, they may suggest 20 white and no black in one bag and 20 black and no white in the other, or 10 white and 10 black in each of the two bags, and so on.
▶ When you are sure they know what to do, leave them to complete the activity sheet working individually.
▶ Children who complete this sheet without difficulty can be given 'Bags and bags of marbles 2' to work on. The number of children playing each marble game on the sheet is shown in the illustration.
▶ Let the children use counting materials to model the activity if they wish. This may help them to recognise the multiplication or division involved.
▶ When they make up their own examples in the second activity, they can devise their own method of recording.

Where next?
▶ If the child completes both activity sheets easily, you will need to try an assessment at a higher level.

TALK ABOUT

▶ 'How do you know how many marbles are needed for this game?'
▶ 'How do you know which marble game is being played here?'
▶ 'In this example you've made up, how many marbles are needed? Why?'

HERE'S THE MATHS

▶ The children can explore as many different ways of filling the bags as they want. They are not asked to find all possible combinations.
▶ Because the marbles in the first activity sheet are to be divided between two bags each time, the children are using subtraction as well as looking at combinations of numbers to 20. For example, if they decide to have seven white marbles in the first bag, they have to work out how many that will leave to go in the other bag: 13. They then have to decide how to arrange the black marbles so that each bag has 20 marbles in total. (Alternatively, they could start with seven white marbles in the first bag, then add on thirteen black marbles, then work out what is left for the second bag.)
▶ After working through the examples of marble-game situations on the second activity sheet, they should be able to construct their own examples. Encourage them to devise examples for each type – that is, ones which involve finding the number of marbles required to play the game, and ones which involve working out which marble game is being played.

IDEAS TO THE RESCUE
MATHS FOCUS – NUMBER KIT 3

Bags and bags of marbles 1

There are 20 white marbles and
20 black marbles in this tin.

They need to be sorted into two bags, 20 marbles in each.
Record some different ways you could fill the two bags.

PHOTOCOPIABLE

IDEAS TO THE RESCUE
MATHS FOCUS – NUMBER KIT 3

11

ASSESSING, USING & APPLYING

PROBLEM SOLVING
◗ Does the child:
• work independently?
• work systematically?
• check results?
• select the appropriate mathematics?
• use materials appropriately?

COMMUNICATION
◗ Does the child:
• record appropriately?
• explain the results?

LOGICAL REASONING
◗ Does the child:
• show understanding of number patterns?
• show understanding of the relationship between multiplication and division?

DIAGNOSTIC ASSESSMENT

Assessing understanding

◗ Look for the following to indicate that the children are ready for **Enrichment activities**. They may:
• work systematically through the first activity sheet, demonstrating a sound understanding of partitioning numbers to 20;
• understand that the first part of the second activity sheet calls for multiplication, and be able to explain why;
• complete the multiplication section without using counting materials, or occasionally use them correctly and with confidence;
• understand that the second part of 'Bags and bags of marbles 2' involves division, and be able to explain why;
• complete the division section without using counting materials, or occasionally use them correctly and with confidence.

◗ Look for the following to indicate that the children are in need of more work on knowing number facts. They may:
• lack confidence in working out the tasks, repeatedly asking questions or seeking reassurance from others in the group;
• need materials for modelling most of the first activity sheet;
• not appreciate the number patterns involved in 'Bags and bags of marbles 1';
• be unable to recognise the multiplication situation, or the division situation, on the second activity sheet;
• use counting materials incorrectly.

Children who need more help

◗ Children who find the activities difficult could try them again, working with lower numbers.

◗ Children who do not have mental recall of number facts to 20 need more opportunities to use counting materials to explore the number patterns involved. **Reinforcement activities** which encourage the learning and quick recall of number facts include '10s and 100s game' (page 18) and 'The wizard's name' (page 26). The **Reinforcement activities** 'Swimming for gold' (page 22), 'Forest lunch' (page 24) and 'Secret of the nines' (page 30) involve exploring patterns in number sequences.

◗ Children who have difficulties with the subtraction aspect need opportunities to develop mental strategies for subtraction. The **Reinforcement activity** 'Cake shop' (page 20) develops one such strategy, that of 'shopkeeper's addition'.

◗ Children who have difficulties with multiplication and division need more practice with continuous addition of small numbers and with simple sharing and grouping situations. The **Reinforcement activity** 'Great motorcycle race 1' (page 28) is suitable for developing mental strategies for division, and 'Back to zero!' (page 16) deals with continuous subtraction.

IDEAS TO THE RESCUE
MATHS FOCUS – NUMBER KIT 3

Name _____

Bags and bags of marbles 2

This is a 2-marble game and 6 children are playing, so they need 12 marbles altogether.

How many marbles are needed for these games?

Marbles needed: ◯   Marbles needed: ◯

Now make up some of your own.

Find out which game is being played by these groups:

4 children, 12 marbles for the group   ◯ -marble game

5 children, 10 marbles for the group   ◯ -marble game

3 children, 15 marbles for the group   ◯ -marble game

Now make up some of your own.

PHOTOCOPIABLE   IDEAS TO THE RESCUE
                                 MATHS FOCUS – NUMBER KIT 3

ASSESSMENT DOUBLE-CHECK

A trip down the street

ASSESSING USING & APPLYING

PROBLEM SOLVING
◗ Does the child:
• know how to tackle the questions?
• select appropriate cards?
• find some or all of the answers?
COMMUNICATION
◗ Does the child:
• communicate effectively in a group situation?
• represent findings in an appropriate way?
LOGICAL REASONING
◗ Does the child:
• organise the work effectively?
• check the work and use approximation to check the reasonableness of answers?

TALK ABOUT

◗ 'In what order did things happen? How do you know?'
◗ 'How did you work that out?'
◗ 'Does that answer seem reasonable?'
◗ 'Are all of the cards needed to answer the questions?'
◗ 'How would you start making up your own cards for a similar puzzle?'

HERE'S THE MATHS

◗ This activity draws on many of the mathematical strategies covered in the **Reinforcement** and **Enrichment activities** in this book.

Key aims
◗ To assess whether the child can:
• extract relevant information;
• operate on the information available;
• select the appropriate mental maths strategies.

What you need
◗ a set of 15 information cards and a set of questions (from the activity sheet) per group (or child)
◗ pencils and paper

Organisation
◗ If the children work as a group, you will need to be with them to assess individual understanding. More confident children could work on their own, with a full set of cards each.
◗ Prepare the cards from the activity sheet beforehand.

The activity
◗ Share the cards randomly among the group.
◗ Ask the children to work out what has happened and to put the cards in order to provide the sequence of events.
◗ Ask the questions from the list on the activity sheet.
◗ Observe the group as they work through the task, and encourage them to record what they do.

Assessing understanding
◗ Look for:
• an ability to select appropriate cards and the appropriate operation to answer each question;
• accuracy in calculating the solutions;
• confidence in switching between mental maths strategies;
• confidence in switching from one context to another.

Where next?
◗ If the children still lack confidence, they will need further **Reinforcement activities** before they move on to tasks which are set in more open-ended contexts and require children to use many different mental maths strategies in the one task, using their knowledge of number facts flexibly.
◗ Children with sound knowledge and understanding can move on to activities in more challenging contexts which use the same mental maths strategies with higher numbers.

IDEAS TO THE RESCUE
MATHS FOCUS – NUMBER KIT 3

A trip down the street

She bought three magazines.	The walk to the shops took five minutes.	The chocolate had caramel inside.
She spent 15 minutes in the shop.	She stopped at her friend Rachel's house on the way home.	The chocolate bars cost 35p each.
She left home at quarter to three.	She bought two bars of chocolate.	She left the house with £5.
She stayed at her friend's house for 25 minutes.	She owed her friend £1.	The magazines cost 99p each.
She gave her friend the £1 she owed.	Rachel's house was on the route from the shop to her home.	The shop was 250m from home.

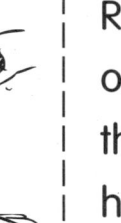

? How far did she walk altogether?
? How much money did she spend?
? What money did she return home with?
? What time did she get home?

REINFORCEMENT ACTIVITY

Back to zero!

Key aims
◗ To explore counting backwards in number sequences.
◗ To use knowledge of number facts to aid an investigation.
◗ To discover factors of a number.
◗ **Also covered:** distinguishing odd from even numbers.

What you need
◗ 1 activity sheet per child
◗ coloured pens
◗ **optional:** number lines for recording; calculators

Introduction
◗ Ask a group of children to sit in a circle. Tell them that they are going to count back in twos, starting from 20. Together clap a beat and go round the circle with the children taking it in turns to call out the next number, on the beat: '20, 18, 16...' Repeat using different starting numbers.

The activity
◗ Give out the activity sheets.
◗ Look at the sequence of jumping back in twos.
◗ Let the children draw in the missing jumps to see for themselves that you end up on zero.
◗ Children who are familiar with using the constant function on a calculator may suggest that you could use that to explore the sequence. (On many calculators, this involves entering 2 4 − 2 = = and then pressing = repeatedly.)
◗ They should then try counting in other jump sizes, starting from the 24 each time and seeing whether they land on zero.
◗ Leave the children to investigate which jump sizes will work, using their own methods for recording what they do.
◗ When they have had time to complete the activity, bring the group back together to discuss the findings. You may want to introduce the term **factors** to them at this point.

Extension ideas
◗ The children could take a number such as 32 and investigate **all** the possible ways of arranging 32 bricks in equal rows, then record their findings.
◗ They could use a longer number line to repeat the main activity with higher numbers such as 36, 60, 72, 100.
◗ Challenge them to record their findings mathematically using any of the four operation symbols. Can they see the division involved?

USING & APPLYING
PROBLEM SOLVING
◗ Work systematically.
COMMUNICATION
◗ Discuss findings using mathematical language.
◗ Record accurately.
LOGICAL REASONING
◗ Predict successful jump sizes.

TALK ABOUT
◗ 'Do you think this jump size will take you back to zero?'
◗ 'How many jumps do you think you will make with that jump size?'
◗ 'Have you found all the possibilities? How do you know?'

HERE'S THE MATHS
◗ In this activity, the children discover the factors of 24: numbers which go into 24 exactly with no remainder.
◗ Some children may use knowledge of number facts to discard some jump sizes (for example, steps of 5) without even testing them out.
◗ The activity involves division by repeated subtraction. Encourage the children to talk about how many jumps are made to direct them to see the division involved.

WHAT TO LOOK FOR
◗ Can the child count back accurately in different jump sizes?
◗ Does the child use knowledge of number facts?

MORE HELP NEEDED
◗ Count back from a smaller number such as 12. Start with counting back in ones, then twos, threes, fours. Discuss why counting back in fives won't work.
◗ Using a large number line to make the jumps physically will help children to see what is going on.

IDEAS TO THE RESCUE
MATHS FOCUS – NUMBER KIT 3

Name _____

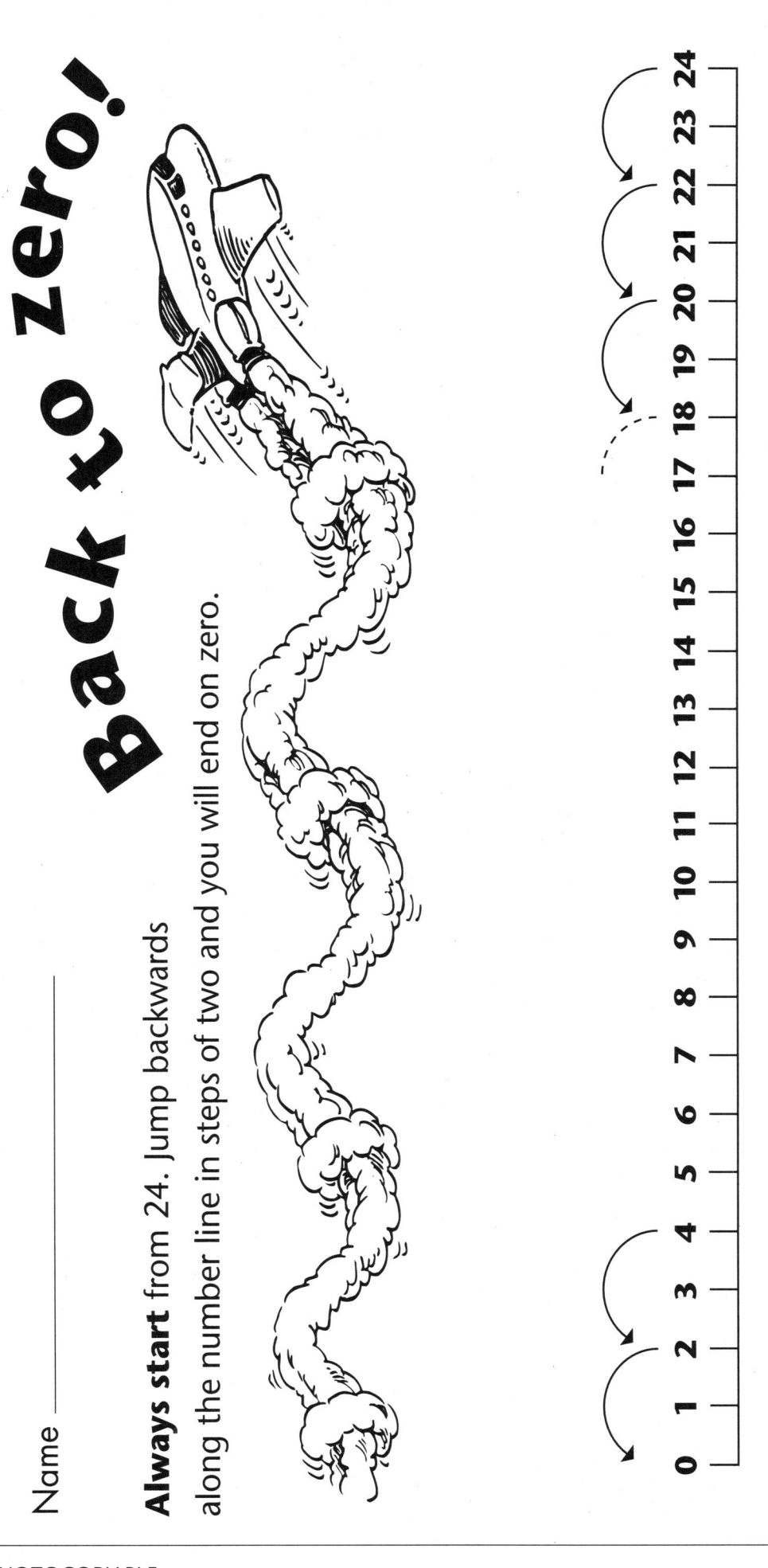

Back to zero!

Always start from 24. Jump backwards along the number line in steps of two and you will end on zero.

0 1 2 3 4 5 6 7 8 9 10 11 12 13 14 15 16 17 18 19 20 21 22 23 24

What if you jump backwards in steps of three? Will you end on zero?
What about steps of four?
Explore for other jump sizes. **How many** different jump sizes are possible?
Record what you do.

PHOTOCOPIABLE

IDEAS TO THE RESCUE
MATHS FOCUS – NUMBER KIT 3

17

USING & APPLYING

PROBLEM SOLVING
◗ Approach the task systematically.
COMMUNICATION
◗ Discuss and account for errors.
LOGICAL REASONING
◗ Understand the reasons for the results and the connections with place value.

TALK ABOUT

◗ 'How many guesses were right?'
◗ 'Did you get better as you went along?'
◗ 'Can you say what will happen to any number when you add 10? What about when you add 100?'

HERE'S THE MATHS

◗ Being able to add and subtract 100 without difficulty shows that the child has an appreciation of place value. Getting children to add and subtract numbers such as 9 and 99 gives you further evidence of their understanding of this concept.

WHAT TO LOOK FOR

◗ Can the child explain how he added on 10?
◗ Can the child carry out the operation immediately in his head?
◗ Can the child explain what she does to subtract 100?

MORE HELP NEEDED

◗ Children finding this activity difficult could use Cuisenaire rods or similar apparatus to model the task each time.

REINFORCEMENT ACTIVITY

10s and 100s game

Key aims
◗ To enhance understanding of place value.
◗ To increase mental agility in adding and subtracting 10s and 100s to/from three-digit numbers.

What you need
◗ 1 activity sheet per pair
◗ 1 set of '10s and 100s' cards per pair (see resource page 44)
◗ 1 calculator per pair (or child)
◗ coloured pens

Organisation
◗ Children should be aware of the effects of adding and subtracting 10s and 100s before they do this activity. You could use the introductory activity to do this, in which case you will need a calculator for each child.

Introduction
◗ Ask the children to display any three-digit number on their calculator, keep adding 10s to it and explain what they notice.
◗ Put another three-digit number on your calculator, keep adding 100s to it and describe what is happening.
◗ Do it again, this time taking away 10s. Then repeat, this time taking away 100s.

The activity
◗ Give each pair a copy of the activity sheet.
◗ Make sure they understand that they must predict the answer before checking with the calculator.
◗ They should both record their turns on the same activity sheet, each using a different-coloured pen from their partner so that they know whose go is which.
◗ Check that they understand the rules. You may want to demonstrate a couple of turns, so that the children are clear about what to record in the table.
◗ Leave them to play the game.

Extension ideas
◗ Children who have completed this activity easily may be ready for activities which involve adding and subtracting 9s and 99s, such as the **Enrichment activity** '999' (page 34).
◗ Play the game again, but this time with a starting number between 4000 and 6000. You could use the 10s and 100s cards again, or make a similar set of 1000s cards.

18 IDEAS TO THE RESCUE
MATHS FOCUS – NUMBER KIT 3

Name _____

10s and 100s game

What you need
- 1 calculator
- pack of 10s and 100s cards

How to play

1 Shuffle the cards and put them in a pile, face down.
2 Make your calculator show a number between 400 and 600.
3 Take turns to pick up the top card and do what it says. If it says −100, you must take a hundred off the number on your calculator, but you must guess the answer and say it aloud before you press the buttons.
4 Keep a record of each go in the table below. Use a different-coloured pen from your partner's, so you know whose go is which.
5 When all the cards have been used, count how many guesses you got right. The player with the most wins.

Start number			
Card	Guess	Calculator number	✓/✗

Player 1 [ ] ✓   Player 2 [ ] ✓

PHOTOCOPIABLE   IDEAS TO THE RESCUE
                                                                                             MATHS FOCUS – NUMBER KIT 3

USING & APPLYING

PROBLEM SOLVING
◗ Develop a mental strategy for subtraction.
COMMUNICATION
◗ Explain how to give the change, using the number line.
LOGICAL REASONING
◗ Appreciate that the more money is spent, the less change there will be.

TALK ABOUT

◗ 'How did you work out the change for this cake?'
◗ 'Do you think this is a good way to work out change?'
◗ 'Which did you find easiest to work out? Why?'
◗ 'Could you work some out in your head now?'

HERE'S THE MATHS

◗ This activity involves children in using a mental method of working out change: adding on from the cost of the item to the amount of money given in payment. This method is also one of the most efficient ways of carrying out any subtraction.

WHAT TO LOOK FOR

◗ Is the child confident working with money?
◗ Does the child add on to find the change?

MORE HELP NEEDED

◗ Children can use coins to model the activity. They can also practise being a 'shopkeeper' giving change, to appreciate how the process works.

REINFORCEMENT ACTIVITY

Cake shop

Key aims
◗ To use 'shopkeeper's addition' (a method of subtraction) to find change from £1.
◗ To use a number line systematically.
◗ To develop a mental strategy for subtraction.

What you need
◗ 1 activity sheet per child
◗ pencils
◗ about £5 in small change
◗ a 0–100 number line per child

Organisation
◗ Have money available (real coins if possible) so that children can check their results.

Introduction
◗ Provide a group of objects each priced at less than £1, and give each child one £1 coin.
◗ Let them take it in turns to choose an object and pay for it with a £1 coin. Show them how you can work out the change using 'shopkeeper's addition' (subtraction). Demonstrate this on a number line.
◗ The children can then take turns at being the shopkeeper, using the number line to help them work out the change.

The activity
◗ Give out the activity sheets. Look at how the baker works out what change to give.
◗ Leave the children to complete the activity sheet, writing the change inside the purses. Let them check their answers using real money.

Extension ideas
◗ Investigate different sets of three cakes which you can buy and still have change from £1.
◗ Take nine cards numbered 11 to 19. Shuffle them and place them face down in a pile. The children work in pairs, with a starting number of 100. They take turns to pick the top card, mentally subtract the number on the card from the starting number, then check their answer on a calculator, returning the card to the bottom of the pile. The first player to reach zero or below wins that round.

IDEAS TO THE RESCUE
MATHS FOCUS – NUMBER KIT 3

Cake shop

Name _____

'One Danish pastry is 39p,
1p more makes 40p, 10p makes 50p
and 50p more makes £1;
so I must give 61p change.'

This is what it looks like on a number line:

1p   +10p   +50p   = 61p change

cost of the cake

How much change would you get from £1 for each of these cakes?

85p, 43p, 64p

19p, 52p, 27p

Write the amount inside the purse.

71p, 38p, 11p

Choose two cakes to buy so you have some change from £1. **How much** change do you have?

PHOTOCOPIABLE

IDEAS TO THE RESCUE
MATHS FOCUS – NUMBER KIT 3

REINFORCEMENT ACTIVITY

Swimming for gold

Key aims
◗ To reinforce the idea of repeated subtraction.
◗ To look for number patterns.

What you need
◗ 1 activity sheet per child
◗ pencils
◗ calculators

Introduction
◗ Talk about how serious swimmers need to practise every day, and gradually become able to swim further and further without resting.
◗ Demonstrate continuous subtraction on a calculator, using the constant function. On some calculators you need to press:
number you want to subtract ⊟ starting number ⊟ and then keep pressing ⊟.
On other calculators you need to press:
number you want to subtract ⊟ starting number ⊟ and then keep pressing ⊟.

The activity
◗ Talk through the activity sheet and make sure the children have a clear picture of what is going on.
◗ Look together at the numbers which have already been filled in: all of January, part of February and the first number for March.
◗ Explain that they are going to find the missing numbers.
◗ Leave them to complete the table and then to fill in the second table on the activity sheet. Explain that for the second table they should invent their own steps.
◗ Encourage the children to check their answers, using the constant function on their calculator, when they have finished.
◗ Discuss with the children how they used number patterns to help them solve the problem.

Extension ideas
◗ Use larger starting numbers and count down with larger intervals such as 10, 9 or 11, all of which give clear patterns.
◗ Plan a six-month programme for swimming 36 lengths a day, so that by the sixth month the swimmer is going more than 10 lengths without stopping.

USING & APPLYING

COMMUNICATION
◗ Describe the number patterns.
LOGICAL REASONING
◗ Use number pattern knowledge to find the missing numbers.

TALK ABOUT
◗ 'What happens to the numbers when you count down in 2s? In 5s?'
◗ 'Are there any patterns when you count down in 3s? In 4s? In 6s?'
◗ 'What happens if you use a different starting number?'
◗ 'Which numbers counted down to zero? Which did not?'

HERE'S THE MATHS
◗ Counting down in even steps provides useful experience of the multiples of a number, and can also help to reinforce the idea of division. For example, the swimmer has 12 resting stops when swimming two lengths at a time: there are 12 lots of 2 in 24; or 24 broken down into steps of 2 gives 12 resting stops.
◗ The second part of the activity provides a more open-ended task, since the children can choose the steps to use each month. They need to find a solution which allows the swimmer to progress at an even pace.

MORE HELP NEEDED
◗ Children having difficulty could use a number line to count down the steps.

IDEAS TO THE RESCUE
MATHS FOCUS – NUMBER KIT 3

Swimming for gold

> I swim 20 lengths every day. For the first month I stopped for a rest after every length, and said '19 lengths to go, 18 lengths to go' and so on.
> For the next month I swam two lengths without stopping, and said '18 lengths to go, 16 lengths to go' and so on. Each month I can swim one more length before resting than the month before. At each rest, I say to myself how many lengths there are to go.

Write down the numbers he called out each month.

January	19	18	17	16	15	14	13	12	11	10	9	8	7	6	5	4	3	2	1
February		18		16		14													
March			17																
April																			
May																			
June																			

> I swim 24 lengths every day. I can also swim longer each month without resting.

Write down the numbers you think she called out each month.

January												
February												
March												
April												
May												
June												

USING & APPLYING

PROBLEM SOLVING
◗ Check answers.
COMMUNICATION
◗ Use language associated with doubling and halving.
◗ Explain how to halve numbers.
LOGICAL REASONING
◗ See that doubling makes a number larger and halving makes it smaller.

TALK ABOUT

◗ 'What do you notice about the results?'
◗ 'How many times bigger than Michael's share is Jonah's share?'
◗ 'Brinda and Jonah always get an even number of things to eat. Why is this?'
◗ 'What fraction of Brinda's share does Michael get?'
◗ 'How are you halving a number?'

HERE'S THE MATHS

◗ Many children confuse doubling with adding 2. The fact that amounts that are doubled are multiplied by 2 can be emphasised practically by using actual items to represent the food.
◗ The children should be aware that doubling a number always gives an even number as the result. Halving a number can give an odd or even number as the result, and may produce halves as well.

WHAT TO LOOK FOR

◗ Can the child halve numbers?
◗ Is the child aware that doubling then doubling again is the same as multiplying by 4?

MORE HELP NEEDED

◗ Use counters or other items to represent the food, so that the children can model the doubling and halving involved.

REINFORCEMENT ACTIVITY

Forest lunch

Key aims
◗ To introduce or to clarify the idea of repeated doubling and halving.
◗ To reinforce flexible use of the two times table.

What you need
◗ 1 activity sheet per child
◗ counting materials such as Multilink

Introduction
◗ Do some mental agility work on doubling and halving with the group. You could start with 1 and go round the group, letting each child double the previous number.
◗ Choose a number, say 200, and let the children take turns to halve it. This may lead to a discussion on how to halve an odd number.

The activity
◗ Go through the activity sheet together, to make sure the children understand the task.
◗ Discuss the language of doubling, including 'two times' and 'twice as much'. Discuss the language of halving, using the words 'sharing' and 'dividing'.
◗ Leave the children to complete the activity sheet. Let them use counting materials to model the task if they want to.

Extension ideas
◗ Introduce other characters – for example, one who eats half as much as Michael or twice as much as Jonah. The children can find out how much of each item these people eat.
◗ Use a supermarket catalogue to set children the task of marking up packets at half price, then working out how many of an item they would get with two packets for the price of one (for example, two packets of biscuits where there are 16 biscuits per packet). They could then try to work out the new price of each biscuit and so on.
◗ Play a game using the postermat and a 1 to 6 dice (or a 10 to 15 dice, if you want the children to work with higher numbers). If you throw an odd number double it, or if you throw an even number halve it, to find out how many spaces to move on that turn. To make a longer track for the game, join together copies of the photocopiable version of the postermat on page 48.

IDEAS TO THE RESCUE
MATHS FOCUS – NUMBER KIT 3

Name _____

Forest lunch

Jonah eats double the amount that Brinda eats and Brinda eats double the amount that Michael eats.
What should be on each plate?

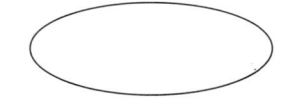

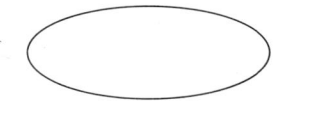

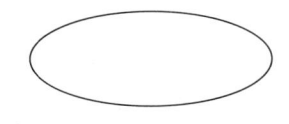

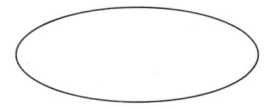

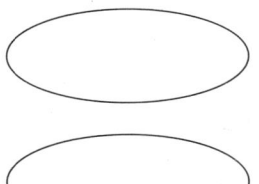

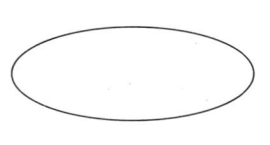

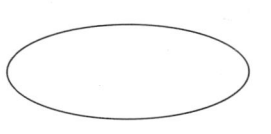

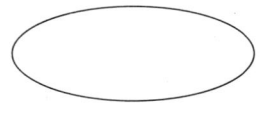

	Michael	Brinda	Jonah
 strawberry	2	4	8
 apple	1		
 biscuit	3		
 bean	10		
 cucumber			12
 chip			20
 plum			16
 chocolate bar			24

Make up some stories about other things that Michael, Brinda and Jonah eat. **Write** on the back of this sheet.

PHOTOCOPIABLE

IDEAS TO THE RESCUE
MATHS FOCUS – NUMBER KIT 3
25

REINFORCEMENT ACTIVITY

The wizard's name

Key aims
◗ To use knowledge of number facts to solve a puzzle.
◗ To use understanding of the four operations to find missing numbers.

What you need
◗ 1 activity sheet per child
◗ pencils and paper
◗ calculators

Introduction
◗ Write out the numbers 13, 25, 14, 1, 13, 5, 9, 19 and show the children the code on the activity sheet. Ask them if they can work out how to use the number code to reveal the message ('my name is').
◗ Once they have understood that 1 gives A, 2 gives B and so on, ask them to write their own name in code.

The activity
◗ Make sure the children understand how the code works.
◗ Remind them to use their knowledge of number facts flexibly – for example, if they know that 4 x 3 = 12, then they also know that 12 ÷ 4 = 3 and 12 ÷ 3 = 4.
◗ Point out that some of the missing numbers are part of a sum and others are part of a number pattern.
◗ Leave them to find the missing numbers and discover the wizard's name. Let them use calculators for checking, if they want to.

Extension ideas
◗ Children can devise their own number codes.
◗ Using one code, make a pack of about ten cards with a word or message in puzzle form on each. Playing in twos or threes, children can take turns to turn over a card. The first one to decode it wins a point.
◗ Make up 'missing number' cards to use with the postermat. Take turns to pick a card and work out how many spaces you can move.

USING & APPLYING

PROBLEM SOLVING
◗ Use own method to find the missing numbers.
◗ Devise own problems.
LOGICAL REASONING
◗ Understand the reasoning behind inverse operations.

TALK ABOUT
◗ 'How did you work out this missing number?'
◗ 'What other ways can you think of that would give the same letter?'

HERE'S THE MATHS
◗ This activity encourages children to use their knowledge of number facts flexibly. For example, some will spot the missing numbers through visualising and others will use inverse operations. You don't need to talk about 'inverse' in a formal way at this stage, since most of the children will be aware of it intuitively: if they know that 4 x 5 = 20, then they can immediately predict that 20 ÷ 5 = 4 and 20 ÷ 4 = 5.

WHAT TO LOOK FOR
◗ Does the child have instant recall of the number facts?
◗ If the child is not recalling number facts to know the answers immediately, can she work them out fairly quickly?
◗ What method is the child using to work out each answer?

MORE HELP NEEDED
◗ Establish which number facts the child is not familiar with and encourage him to say how he is arriving at the answers. Remind him of other activities where he has experienced a particular number pattern before.

IDEAS TO THE RESCUE
MATHS FOCUS – NUMBER KIT 3

The wizard's name

Name _____

Here is a code.

1	2	3	4	5	6	7	8	9	10	11	12	13	14	15	16	17	18	19	20	21	22	23	24	25	26
A	B	C	D	E	F	G	H	I	J	K	L	M	N	O	P	Q	R	S	T	U	V	W	X	Y	Z

Find the numbers that go in the spaces below. Use the code to make the wizard's name appear!

20 − ☐ = 1

3, 6, ☐ ,12,15

☐ ÷ 4 = 5

☐ × 4 = 16

2, 4, 6, ☐ ,10

7 + 7 = ☐

☐ ,10,15,20,25

5 × 5 = ☐

20 − ☐ = 17

20 − ☐ = 4

2 × ☐ = 10

15 + ☐ = 20

3 + ☐ = 15

☐ ÷ 4 = 3

20, ☐ ,16,14,12

19 − ☐ = 6

12 × ☐ = 12

20 − 9 = ☐

19 − ☐ = 14

Make up your own mystery messages using number puzzles and the code.

USING & APPLYING

PROBLEM SOLVING
◗ Check the answers.
COMMUNICATION
◗ Discuss disputed answers before checking.
◗ Use mathematical language correctly.
LOGICAL REASONING
◗ Use number pattern knowledge to assist mental recall of number facts.

TALK ABOUT

◗ 'How did you work out the answer for this card?'
◗ 'Has he given the correct answer?'
◗ 'How can multiplication help you find the answer?'

HERE'S THE MATHS

◗ This game provides a useful way of practising number skills. Knowledge of multiplication facts is invaluable for carrying out division, since they are inverse operations. For example, to work out $32 \div 4$, the child can use the associated fact that $4 \times 8 = 32$ to give 8 as the answer. For $72 \div 4$, encourage the child to see 72 as $40 + 32$ so that the answer can be worked out as $10 + 8$ or 18.

WHAT TO LOOK FOR

◗ Does the child use multiplication facts confidently to work out the division?
◗ Does the child see the relationship between multiplication and division?

MORE HELP NEEDED

◗ Children who have difficulty with the division problems need more practice in grouping and sharing with counting materials. They could play the game using the calculator throughout, to become more familiar with how division works.

REINFORCEMENT ACTIVITY

Great motorcycle race 1

Key aims
◗ To reinforce understanding of division.
◗ To practise mental recall of division facts.

What you need
◗ 1 postermat (or copy of resource page 48) per group
◗ a set of 'Great motorcycle race 1' cards (resource page 45) per group
◗ 1 counter per child
◗ 1 calculator per group

Organisation
◗ Prepare the 'Great motorcycle race 1' cards, preferably mounting each set on card before cutting them out.
◗ This activity assumes that children are already familiar with the division operation sign ($\div$).
◗ Some children may be confident enough to work out the game on their own, using the rules sheet opposite.
◗ Use the photocopiable version of the postermat (page 48) to allow more groups to play at one time.

Introduction
◗ Remind the children of the number patterns involved in multiplication tables. This will help them to recall answers mentally when they play the game.

The activity
◗ Go over the rules of the game with the children.
◗ Explain that they can use the calculator to check an opponent's answer if they disagree with it.
◗ Leave them to play the game.

Extension ideas
◗ Devise more playing cards and change the rules.
◗ Play the game using two dice, such as a 2, 3, 4 dice and a 12, 24, 36, 48, 60, 72 dice. Take turns to throw both the dice, divide the larger number by the smaller and add the digits of the answer together to tell you how many spaces to move. For example, if you throw 72 and 4, you move forward 9 spaces. Choose dice appropriate to the practice you want to give to specific children. Join copies of the photocopiable version of the postermat together to create a longer track.
◗ Invent a new game using the postermat.
◗ Go on to play 'The great motorcycle race 2' (page 40).

IDEAS TO THE RESCUE
MATHS FOCUS – NUMBER KIT 3

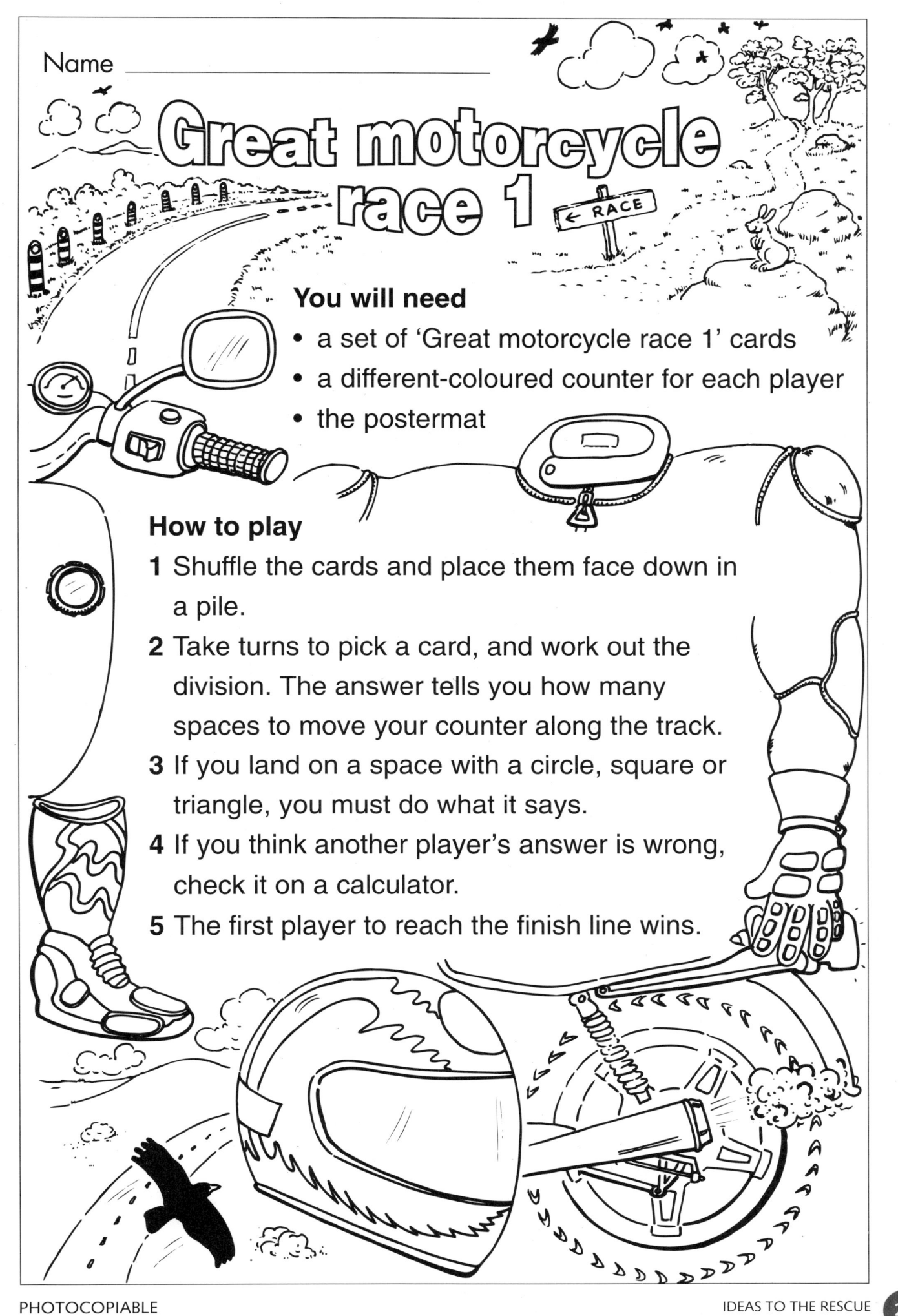

Name _____

Great motorcycle race 1

You will need
- a set of 'Great motorcycle race 1' cards
- a different-coloured counter for each player
- the postermat

How to play

1 Shuffle the cards and place them face down in a pile.
2 Take turns to pick a card, and work out the division. The answer tells you how many spaces to move your counter along the track.
3 If you land on a space with a circle, square or triangle, you must do what it says.
4 If you think another player's answer is wrong, check it on a calculator.
5 The first player to reach the finish line wins.

REINFORCEMENT ACTIVITY

Secret of the nines

Key aims
◗ To discover a strategy relating to division by 9.
◗ To use knowledge of division.

What you need
◗ 1 activity sheet per child
◗ paper and pencils
◗ calculators

The activity
◗ Give out the activity sheets.
◗ Talk through the example given.
◗ Encourage the children to use mental maths to work out numbers which divide exactly by 9, but have calculators available for those who want to use them.
◗ When you are sure the children know what to do, leave them to complete the activity.

Extension ideas
◗ Use the strategy to discover which three-digit numbers within the range 300–350, for example, are divisible by 9 with no remainder.
◗ Play a version of Pelmanism using cards with a selection of two-digit, three-digit and four-digit numbers, including ones which divide by 9 and ones which don't. Spread out the cards face down. Take turns to turn over any two cards. If the two numbers both have the same number of digits, and are both divisible by 9 with no remainder, keep the pair. If not, turn them back over. Continue until no more pairs are available.

USING & APPLYING

PROBLEM SOLVING
◗ Use mental maths to find numbers divisible by 9 with no remainder.
◗ Organise the task to work systematically.
COMMUNICATION
◗ Record accurately.
◗ Explain any findings.
LOGICAL REASONING
◗ Spot a pattern in the numbers.

TALK ABOUT
◗ 'How did you find out whether this number divides by 9 with no remainder?'
◗ 'What do its digits add up to?'
◗ 'Which number will you try next?'
◗ 'Can you see a pattern in these numbers? Is there anything they all have in common?'
◗ 'Does this work with all numbers?'

HERE'S THE MATHS
◗ The children will discover that if a number's digits add up to 9 then the number itself will divide by 9 exactly. So, for example, they can say immediately that 612 will divide by 9 with no remainder.

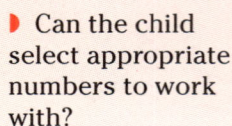

WHAT TO LOOK FOR
◗ Can the child select appropriate numbers to work with?
◗ Can the child spot what the numbers have in common?
◗ Can the child suggest how this knowledge might be useful?

Name _____

Secret of the nines

I've discovered a secret about dividing by 9. It means I can always know whether a number will divide by 9 or not.

Find a number which divides by nine exactly.

I've found 18.

Add up the digits of that number.

1 + 8 gives 9.

Record the result.

Do this for other numbers which divide by 9 exactly.

Include numbers bigger than 100.

Keep going until you discover the secret.

divides by 9 exactly	digits add up to

The secret is:

PHOTOCOPIABLE

IDEAS TO THE RESCUE
MATHS FOCUS – NUMBER KIT 3

ENRICHMENT ACTIVITY

Spend! Spend! Spend!

Key aims
◗ To consolidate mental subtraction using knowledge of number facts.
◗ To carry out calculations involving money and decimal notation.
◗ To provide an opportunity for individual recording.

What you need
◗ 1 activity sheet per child
◗ pencils and blank paper
◗ **optional:** calculators

The activity
◗ Go through the activity sheet with the group.
◗ Encourage the children to make quick calculations in their heads of the total cost of the items they choose.
◗ Leave them to explore different ways they could spend their £5 for a month.
◗ Provide blank paper for recording. Stress that careful and systematic recording is important, but let them decide how to do this.
◗ When they have finished let them check their work on a calculator if they want to.
◗ Bring the group back together to discuss what they have done and to compare methods. Challenge them to choose any four items that they would like and give a quick and approximate estimation of what they add up to.
◗ This activity requires children to decide on their method of recording. Asking them questions about what they have done will help to show how efficient their method is.

Extension ideas
◗ Provide the children with a high street shop catalogue. Tell them they have £20 to plan a party for a few friends. Working in pairs with a timer and a selection of priced-up items, the children take turns to select three, four or five items for their partner to buy. Their partner must give a reasonable estimate of the cost of these items within 30 seconds, and then make an accurate calculation within a longer agreed time span.

USING & APPLYING

PROBLEM SOLVING
◗ Work systematically.
◗ Develop mental strategies.
◗ Check results.
COMMUNICATION
◗ Discuss the work.
◗ Record clearly and systematically.

TALK ABOUT

◗ 'How will you record this?'
◗ 'How will you check your work?'
◗ 'How much do these things cost altogether? How much of this month's £5 have you not spent?'
◗ 'Which month did you have most change left over?'
◗ 'Which is the best way of doing the addition?'
◗ 'Can you spend £5 exactly?'

HERE'S THE MATHS

◗ Most children will use the 'shopkeeper's addition' method for finding change. For example, to find change from £5 for an item costing £4.40, they will say '... and 10p makes £4.50 and 50p makes £5; that gives 60p change'.
◗ Being able to give a quick approximation of the cost of a number of items is a useful skill in everyday life. To give an approximation, children could mentally round each item up to or down to the nearest pound (for example £1.25 + £2.60 is approximately £1 + £3).

WHAT TO LOOK FOR

◗ Is the child confident with decimal notation?
◗ Can the child give a quick approximation of the total cost?

MORE HELP NEEDED

◗ Discuss possible mental strategies.
◗ Use real coins to model the activity.

IDEAS TO THE RESCUE
MATHS FOCUS – NUMBER KIT 3

Name _____

Spend! Spend! Spend!

You have £5 a month to spend on items from this catalogue.

What will you choose?
What will you spend the £5 on next month?
What might your friend choose?

Make choices for other months.
Record what you do.

PHOTOCOPIABLE

IDEAS TO THE RESCUE
MATHS FOCUS – NUMBER KIT 3

ENRICHMENT ACTIVITY

999

USING & APPLYING

PROBLEM SOLVING
◗ Apply known strategies.
COMMUNICATION
◗ Discuss mental methods used.

TALK ABOUT

◗ 'How did you work this out in your head?'
◗ 'How will you work out 292 + 9?'

HERE'S THE MATHS

◗ To become proficient at mental maths, children should become used to adapting the number facts they already know to a new task. For some children, adding 8 is quickly done by adding 10 and then subtracting 2; others might approach it by adding 5 and then adding 3. Adding (or subtracting) 11 is usually done by adding the 10 and then adding 1.

WHAT TO LOOK FOR

◗ Can the child use a variety of mental methods?
◗ Can the child explain how she carried out a calculation?

MORE HELP NEEDED

◗ Practise adding and subtracting 10 until the children can do this with confidence. Then move on to adding 9 and 11, showing them that it involves adding the 10 and then adding/subtracting 1.
◗ Give them a list of numbers, to which they add 99 to find the result in each case. They can then compare the 'before' and 'after' numbers to see what they notice, and discover for themselves that adding 100 then subtracting 1 would give the same result.

Key aim
◗ To develop and use mental strategies for adding 9 and 99 to, and subtracting them from, three-digit numbers.

What you need
◗ 1 activity sheet per pair
◗ coloured counters
◗ 1 set of '999' operation cards and 1 set of '999' number cards per pair (resource sheet on page 46)
◗ 1 calculator per pair
◗ a 1, 2, 3 dice per pair

Organisation
◗ For each pair, prepare two sets of the '999' operation cards shuffled in one pile and two sets of the '999' number cards shuffled and put in a second pile. Mount them on card and cover with sticky-back plastic to make them more durable.

Introduction
◗ Remind the children how 9 and 99 can easily be added or subtracted mentally by adding or subtracting 10 or 100 and adjusting by 1.
◗ Work through some examples together, to make sure they are all confident with this. For example, 'To do 127 – 9, you take 10 from 127 which gives 117 and then add the 1 which gives 118.'

The activity
◗ Give each pair a copy of the activity sheet and go over the rules of the game.
◗ Make sure they realise that if they land on a star, they should pick one card from the top of each of the two piles. If, for example, they pick –9 and 625, they then take 9 away from 625.
◗ Leave them to play the game.

Extension ideas
◗ Add a set of +29/–29/+39/–39 cards to the operation pack and play the game again.
◗ Investigate strategies for adding and subtracting 8 or 88, 7 or 77, 11 or 101 by exploring what happens when you add or subtract these numbers.

999

What you need
game track below
1 counter each
(different colours)
1–3 dice
both packs of 999 cards

How to play
1 Shuffle each pack of cards and put the cards face down, in separate packs.
2 Take turns to throw the dice and move along the track. If you land on a star, take one card from the top of each pack.
3 One card will have a number in the hundreds. The other will tell you what to do with it.
4 Work out and say the answer.
5 Check it on the calculator.
If you were right, move on one space. If not, go back one.
6 The first player to reach the finish wins.

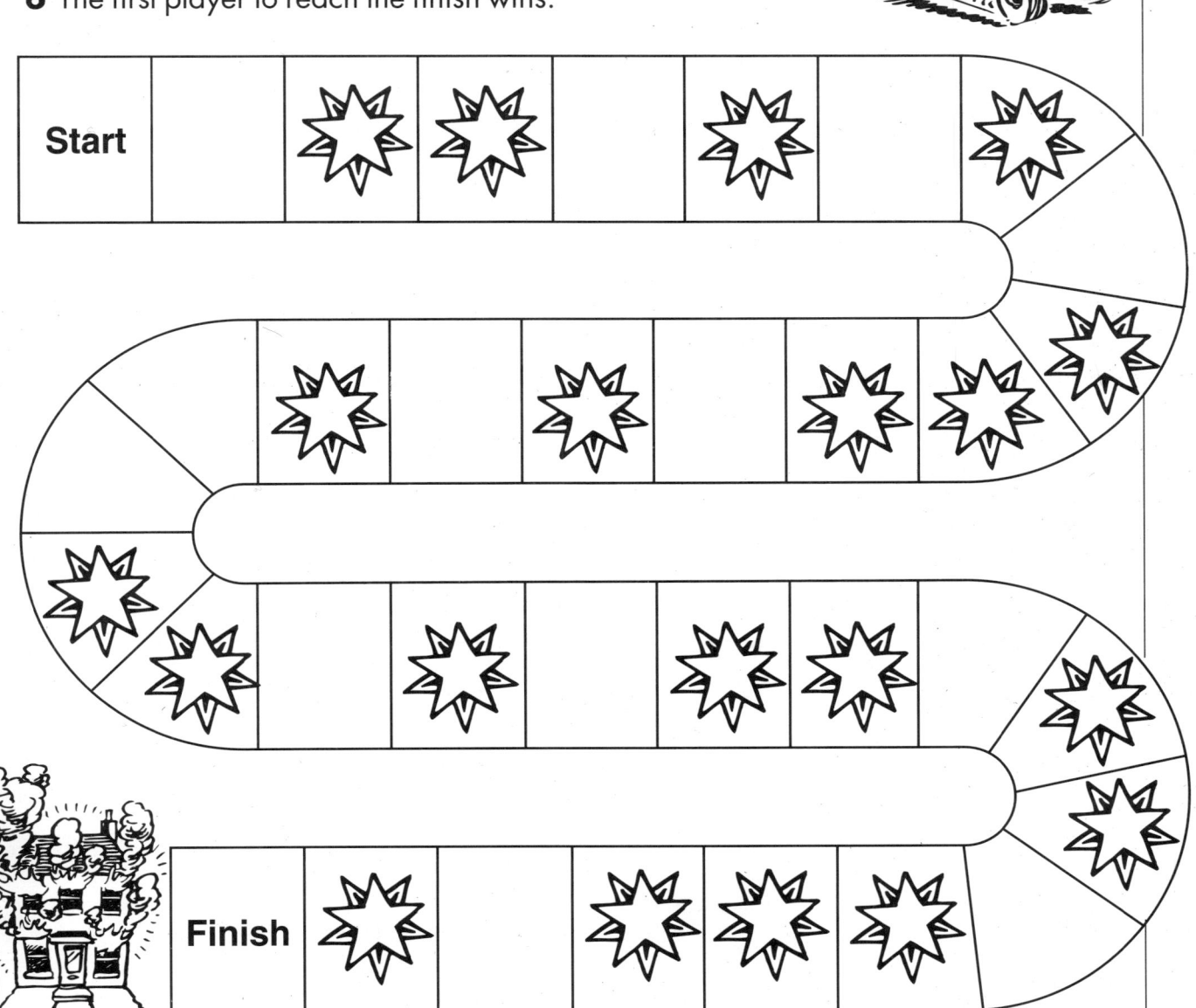

Start

Finish

PHOTOCOPIABLE

IDEAS TO THE RESCUE
MATHS FOCUS – NUMBER KIT 3

ENRICHMENT ACTIVITY

Easter at Exeter Street

Key aims
◗ To consolidate mental addition involving numbers less than 100.
◗ To use number facts in a problem-solving context.
◗ To devise methods of recording.

What you need
◗ 1 activity sheet per child
◗ pencils and paper
◗ *Christmas in Exeter Street* by Diana Hendry (Walker Books, 1991)
◗ **optional:** calculators

Organisation
◗ Have calculators available, but not given out individually.
◗ The children may want to use extra copies of the street plan on the activity sheet for their recording.

Introduction
◗ To provide a context for the activity, read *Christmas in Exeter Street* by Diana Hendry: a story about all the people and animals that came to stay with the Mistletoe family.

The activity
◗ Give out the activity sheets. You may want to look together at what is involved.
◗ Let the children use calculators to check their addition if they want to, but encourage them to work out each addition in their heads first.
◗ Stress the need for careful recording of the routes tried.
◗ Leave the children to work on their own. Putting a time limit on the activity could encourage them to think ahead.
◗ Encourage them to discuss with the group the strategies they used to find the correct route.
◗ Describing their range of techniques for mental calculations allows children to share and consolidate their understanding of strategies and to learn new ones from others in the group.

Extension ideas
◗ Using the story book, find various ways to stow all the animals in the Exeter Street house.
◗ Devise a road network between six towns and write in the number of kilometres for each road, then investigate the lengths of various journeys.

USING & APPLYING

PROBLEM SOLVING
◗ Work systematically.
◗ Use and develop mental strategies.
◗ Check results.
COMMUNICATION
◗ Discuss the work.
◗ Record clearly and systematically.
LOGICAL REASONING
◗ Think ahead to reach the solution more quickly.

TALK ABOUT
◗ 'How did you find the route that Mrs Mistletoe took?'
◗ 'Which is the route giving the smallest/largest number of animals?'
◗ 'How many different routes can you find?'

HERE'S THE MATHS
◗ By thinking ahead, the children can abandon totals that they see will be too big or too small.
◗ They will see the importance of working systematically and recording what they do in finding the solution. Using logical reasoning skills will help them to reach the solution more effectively through trial and improvement.
◗ This is the correct route: Upper Exeter St, West St, Wells St, Short St, Church St, East St, Lower Exeter St.

WHAT TO LOOK FOR
◗ Is the child sure of the total she is aiming at?
◗ Does the child try several different routes?
◗ Does the child realise fairly soon that some routes will give too many pets and others too few?

MORE HELP NEEDED
◗ Create a similar activity which involves smaller numbers.

Name _____

Easter at Exeter Street

The Mistletoe family enjoyed having their house full at Christmas so much that Mrs Mistletoe decided to go for a walk and knock on doors, asking people if they would like her to look after their animals while they went away for Easter.

By the time she got back home, she had 54 pets to look after. She did not go along any street more than once, and no-one was out when she called.

Find out from the plan which walk she took and **record** it. The numbers tell you how many animals are in each street.

Streets on plan:
- Upper Exeter St. 17
- Lower Exeter St. 9
- Long St. 19
- Green St. 10
- West St. 3
- East St. 11
- Wells St. 4
- Bath St. 1
- Short St. 7
- Church St. 3
- Lyme St. 2
- Park St. 6
- High St. 8

Find out how many animals she would have collected on other walks.
Record what you do.
Which walk gives the most animals?
Which walk gives the fewest animals?

PHOTOCOPIABLE

IDEAS TO THE RESCUE
MATHS FOCUS – NUMBER KIT 3

37

ENRICHMENT ACTIVITY

Kiosk on the beach

Key aims
▶ To appreciate the number pattern involved in the continuous addition of 99.
▶ To use this to develop mental strategies for multiplying 99 and 199 by numbers less than 10.

What you need
▶ 1 activity sheet per child
▶ pencils
▶ **optional:** calculators

Organisation
▶ Have calculators available for checking.

The activity
▶ Go through the activity sheet with the children. Make sure they understand the method for working out multiples of 99.
▶ Explain that they are to do the working out in their heads. They can use the calculator to check their work when they have finished (if they want to).
▶ Leave them to complete the activity sheet individually.
▶ When they have had time to work on the task, bring the group back together to discuss when this type of multiplication could be useful in real life.

Extension ideas
▶ Adapt the strategy to use with other numbers, such as multiples of 98 or 19.
▶ Think of easy methods for multiplying other numbers, such as 25p (using 4 x 25p = £1), 75p (as 50p plus 25p) and 81p (as 80p plus 1p). Write out these methods for others to use.

USING & APPLYING

PROBLEM SOLVING
▶ Use the mental strategy given to work out the bills.
COMMUNICATION
▶ Discuss the work.
▶ Record clearly.
LOGICAL REASONING
▶ Know when an answer is reasonable or not.

TALK ABOUT
▶ 'How did you work out the total cost of these sun-hats?'
▶ 'How would you multiply £1.99 by a number?'
▶ 'What bills have you worked out for the cloth hats?'

HERE'S THE MATHS
▶ Since many items are priced just short of a number of pounds, this activity will give children a mental strategy which is useful in many everyday situations.

WHAT TO LOOK FOR
▶ Can the child explain what to do to find multiples of 99?
▶ Can the child use the strategy with confidence to work out higher multiples?
▶ Can the child adapt the strategy to work out multiples of 199?

MORE HELP NEEDED
▶ Children who find the activity difficult need to work with structural materials in base 10, so that they understand and can visualise the logic underlying the multiplication strategy.

IDEAS TO THE RESCUE
MATHS FOCUS – NUMBER KIT 3

Name _____

Kiosk on the beach

All cloth hats £1.99p

All paper sun-hats 99p

I've found an easy way to work out in my head the cost of any number of paper sun-hats:
1 × 99 is the same as 100 − 1.
One paper sun-hat costs 99p.
2 × 99 is the same as 200 − 2.
So the cost of two paper sun-hats is 198p or £1.98 – and so on.

Work out these bills in your head:

99p each Cost:

99p each Cost:

99p each Cost:

99p each Cost:

Now think of a quick way of multiplying £1.99 by any number.
Work out some bills for cloth sun-hats.

PHOTOCOPIABLE

IDEAS TO THE RESCUE
MATHS FOCUS – NUMBER KIT 3

USING & APPLYING

PROBLEM SOLVING
◗ Use counting materials to check answers.

COMMUNICATION
◗ Discuss disputed answers before checking.
◗ Use appropriate mathematical language.

LOGICAL REASONING
◗ Use number pattern knowledge to assist mental recall of number facts.

TALK ABOUT

◗ 'How did you work out the remainder for this one?'
◗ 'Do you think this one will give a large or small remainder?'
◗ 'What strategies do you use to calculate the remainders?'
◗ 'Why would a calculator be no help?'

HERE'S THE MATHS

◗ Children will have come across the idea of remainders early on from their experiences of sharing. When they are working out a division, encourage the children to visualise the items being shared between people. The number left over at the end is the remainder.

WHAT TO LOOK FOR

◗ Is the child confident with the idea of a remainder?
◗ Does the child show an ability to visualise the sharing process?

MORE HELP NEEDED

◗ To help children calculate remainders mentally, give them division activities with counting materials and ask them to record the results. Talk about their results and then encourage them to reconstruct in their heads what they have just done.

ENRICHMENT ACTIVITY

Great motorcycle race 2

Key aims
◗ To enhance understanding of division with remainders.
◗ To encourage children to develop mental strategies for calculating remainders.

What you need
◗ 1 postermat (or copy of resource sheet on page 48) per group
◗ 1 set of 'Great motorcycle race 2' cards (resource sheet on page 47) per group
◗ 1 activity sheet per group
◗ coloured counters
◗ counting materials

Organisation
◗ Prepare the 'Great motorcycle race 2' cards using one or more photocopies of page 47.
◗ Have counting materials readily available.
◗ Use copies of the photocopiable version of the postermat on page 48 to allow more children to do the activity at the same time.

Introduction
◗ Remind the children of the idea of remainders by exploring practically. For example, give each child 10 objects and ask her to share them between two people, then three, then four, then five. Discuss the results.

The activity
◗ Give each group a copy of the activity sheet, the postermat, one counter each and a set of the 'Great motorcycle race 2' cards.
◗ Go over the rules of the game. Explain that they can use the counting materials to check the answers if they are uncertain.
◗ When you are sure they understand the rules, leave them to play the game.

Extension ideas
◗ Make up more difficult division cards and devise new rules for playing. (Larger remainders would mean making a larger track by joining together copies of resource page 48.)
◗ Investigate what numbers would give a remainder of 2 when divided by 5, or what numbers would give a remainder of 9 when divided by 10. Record on a number line or 100 square.

Name _____

Great motorcycle race 2

You will need
a set of 'Great motorcycle race 2' cards
a different-coloured counter for each player
a postermat

How to play
1 Shuffle the cards and place them face down in a pile.
2 Take turns to pick a card from the top of the pile and work out the calculation.
3 The remainder tells you how many spaces to move your counter along the track. If there is no remainder, you stay where you are.
4 If you land on a space with a circle, square or triangle, you must do what it says.
5 The first player to reach the finish line wins.

PHOTOCOPIABLE

IDEAS TO THE RESCUE
MATHS FOCUS – NUMBER KIT 3

ENRICHMENT ACTIVITY

Target practice

Key aims
- To develop mental strategies for doubling, halving and trebling.
- To develop problem-solving methods.

What you need
- 1 activity sheet per pair
- coloured pens
- a piece of cloth (for a blindfold) per pair
- calculators

Organisation
- The children could cut out their target board and mount it on thick corrugated card before they begin taking their 'shots'.

The activity
- Give out the activity sheets and make sure the children understand what to do.
- Each player will need a different-coloured pen, so that they can distinguish whose 'shots' are which.
- You may want to work out the score for three shots together, so that the children understand the scoring method and are clear about how halving, doubling and trebling are involved.
- Encourage them to work out the halving, doubling and trebling mentally, but if they want to, let them use calculators for the final addition to work out the total score.
- It is important to encourage the children to talk about their strategies – they can adopt new ones if they think these are more efficient than the method they have used.

Extension ideas
- Investigate mental methods for scoring more difficult numbers on the target board, such as double 17 and treble 28.
- Find out how these scores could be made with three shots: 83; 93; 88. Investigate whether there is more than one way to make the same score.
- Use the postermat, a double/halve/treble dice and a 16/18/20/22/24/26 dice (for example). Take turns to throw the two dice, find the answer and then use the highest digit of that number to tell you how many spaces to move. For example, 'treble' and '26' gives 78, so move forward 8 spaces. First player to the finish wins.

USING & APPLYING

PROBLEM SOLVING
- Devise own strategies.
- Work systematically.
- Check scores.

COMMUNICATION
- Discuss strategies used.
- Record clearly.

LOGICAL REASONING
- Recognise the number patterns involved.

TALK ABOUT
- 'How did you work out the score for this shot?'
- 'How do you treble a number?'
- 'What is the highest score possible?'

HERE'S THE MATHS
- There are different strategies that the children could use. For example, for trebling they may say: 'Treble 21 is three 20s plus 3', or 'I know that three 11s are 33', or 'Three 19s are three 20s take away 3'.

WHAT TO LOOK FOR
- Can the child double and treble numbers quickly?
- Which number facts does the child know immediately by recall?
- Can the child explain the method of calculation used?

MORE HELP NEEDED
- Children who have difficulty working out the score for each shot need more practice with doubling and trebling small numbers and then looking at what happens when you double and treble multiples of 10.

IDEAS TO THE RESCUE
MATHS FOCUS – NUMBER KIT 3

Name _____

Target practice

How to play
Take turns to wear a blindfold.
Use your pen to touch the target board and score points.
The outer ring scores **half** the number.
The middle ring scores **double** the number.
The inner ring scores **treble** the number.

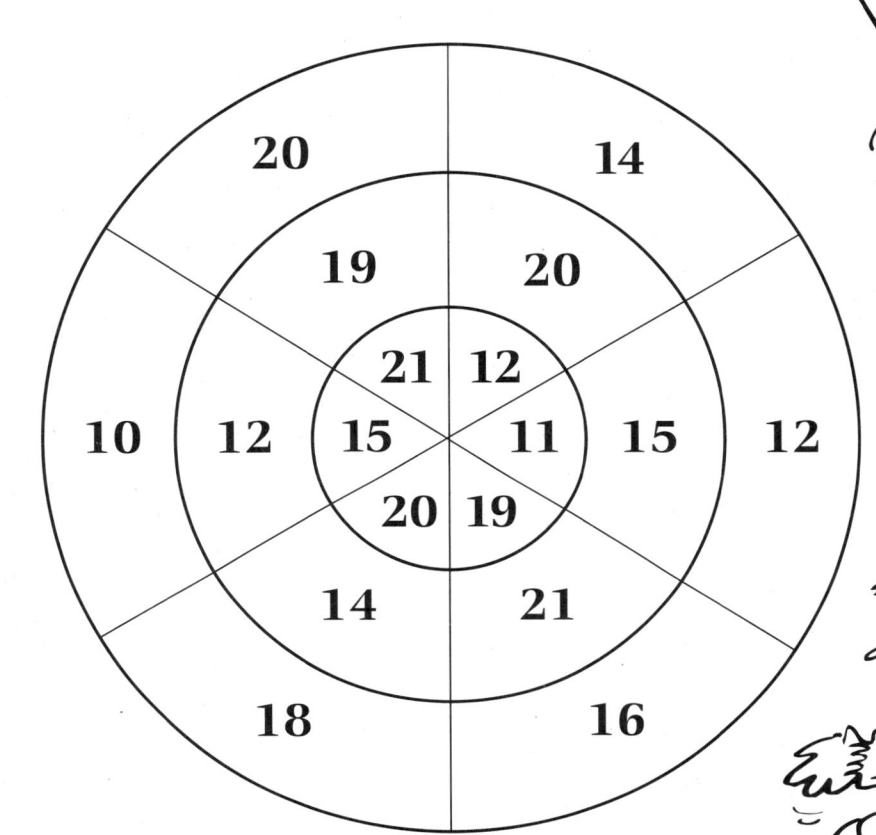

Have three goes.
Remove the blindfold and see what you have scored.

Target board numbers:
- 20, 14 (outer top)
- 19, 20 (middle upper)
- 21, 12 (inner)
- 15, 11 (inner)
- 20, 19 (inner)
- 10, 12, 15, 12 (middle row)
- 14, 21 (middle lower)
- 18, 16 (outer bottom)

Record your scores.
Work out the total score for that go.

Name	1st shot	2nd shot	3rd shot	total score

PHOTOCOPIABLE

IDEAS TO THE RESCUE
MATHS FOCUS – NUMBER KIT 3
43

+10	−10	+100	−100
+10	−10	+100	−100
+10	−10	+100	−100
+10	−10	+100	−100

IDEAS TO THE RESCUE
MATHS FOCUS – NUMBER KIT 3

PHOTOCOPIABLE

Great motorcycle race 1

15 ÷ 5	10 ÷ 2	16 ÷ 4
20 ÷ 10	9 ÷ 3	5 ÷ 5
12 ÷ 3	40 ÷ 10	16 ÷ 8
14 ÷ 7	12 ÷ 2	10 ÷ 10
30 ÷ 10	25 ÷ 5	12 ÷ 6
15 ÷ 3	4 ÷ 4	20 ÷ 5

PHOTOCOPIABLE

IDEAS TO THE RESCUE
MATHS FOCUS – NUMBER KIT 3

−9	+9	−99	+99
−9	+9	−99	+99
−9	+9	−99	+99
−9	+9	−99	+99

243	478	625	187
814	529	716	292
375	286	127	431
564	849	517	794

Great motorcycle race 2

7 ÷ 4	8 ÷ 5	24 ÷ 5
19 ÷ 2	20 ÷ 5	14 ÷ 3
15 ÷ 2	18 ÷ 4	17 ÷ 4
15 ÷ 3	19 ÷ 5	17 ÷ 5
13 ÷ 5	20 ÷ 3	25 ÷ 10
64 ÷ 10	41 ÷ 10	13 ÷ 4

PHOTOCOPIABLE

SEE PAGES 24, 26, 28, 40 AND 42

The Great Motorcycle Race

Start

Finish

○ Pit stop / Miss a turn

□ You have overtaken / Go forward 1

△ Engine trouble / Go back 1

48 IDEAS TO THE RESCUE
MATHS FOCUS – NUMBER KIT 3

PHOTOCOPIABLE